Deep Trouble

LEVEL ONE   400 HEADWORDS

OXFORD
UNIVERSITY PRESS

Great Clarendon Street, Oxford OX2 6DP

Oxford University Press is a department of the University of Oxford.
It furthers the University's objective of excellence in research, scholarship,
and education by publishing worldwide in

Oxford New York

Auckland Cape Town Dar es Salaam Hong Kong Karachi
Kuala Lumpur Madrid Melbourne Mexico City Nairobi
New Delhi Shanghai Taipei Toronto

With offices in

Argentina Austria Brazil Chile Czech Republic France Greece
Guatemala Hungary Italy Japan Poland Portugal Singapore
South Korea Switzerland Thailand Turkey Ukraine Vietnam

OXFORD and OXFORD ENGLISH are registered trade marks of
Oxford University Press in the UK and in certain other countries

First published in Dominoes 2004

2016 2015

10

ISBN: 978 0 19 424761 0 BOOK
ISBN: 978 0 19 424725 2 BOOK AND MULTIROM PACK
MULTIROM NOT AVAILABLE SEPARATELY

Printed in China

This book is printed on paper from certified and well-managed sources.

ACKNOWLEDGEMENTS

The publisher would like to thank the following for their time and assistance during the photoshoot: Dan
Hughes at Port Solent Marina, Port Solent, Portsmouth; The Portsmouth Marriot Hotel;
Mark Allen at Lymington Motor Boat Charter (www.lymingtoncharter.co.uk)

With special thanks to: the models from MPA Bournemouth: Ashley Courier, Steve Fitzakerley,
Laura Greany, Neil May and Sharon Rumsey

Commissioned Photography by: Chris King

The publisher would like to thank the following for permission to reproduce photographs: Alamy
Images pp iv (men holding guns/Photofusion Picture Library), 44 (Street scene/geogphotos);
Corbis pp iv (Police officers/Wally McNamee), 7 (College building/Danny Lehman), 12
(Push/Patrik Giardino), 39 (Diver/Stephen Frink), 42 (Bird watching/Macduff Everton), 43
(Junkanoo parade/Philip Gould), 44 (Victoria, Seychelles/Hubert Stadler); Getty Images pp iv
(Lear jet in flight/Quandrant Picture Lib), 24 (Diver/Zac Macaulay); Masterfile pp 7 (Ocean
waves/Mike Dobel), 12 (Baseball player/Zoran Milch), 42 (Sailing/Dale Sanders); OUP pp iv
(Shark/Ingram), 12 (Man shouting/Stockbyte), 19 (Tropical beach/Photodisc), 25 (Beach/
Photodisc), 30 (Money/Photodisc), 42 (Fishing/Photodisc), 42 (Windsurfing/Jupiter Images/
Brand X), 42 (Golf/Photodisc), 42 (Surfing/Corel), 43 (Snorkelling/Photodisc), 43 (Palm trees
by ocean/Photodisc).

The Activities and Projects in this book were written by Christine Lindop

DOMINOES

Series Editors: Bill Bowler and Sue Parminter

Deep Trouble

Lesley Thompson

Illustrated by Sebastian Camagajevac

Lesley Thompson was born in Newcastle upon Tyne, in the north of England, but she moved to Spain some years ago, and now lives near Alicante. She loves reading, the cinema, music, laughing with her friends, and looking at the sea. She also enjoys walking in the countryside in England and Spain, and one day she hopes to walk the *Camino de Santiago*, in northern Spain. Lesley has also adapted *The Secret Agent* in the Dominoes series.

OXFORD
UNIVERSITY PRESS

BEFORE READING

1 Here are some of the people in the story *Deep Trouble*. Who is good and who is bad? Write *good* or *bad*.

Amy

Brad

Matt

Sharon

Troy

. . . .

2 *Deep trouble* means 'very big problems'. What are the problems in this story? Tick two boxes.

a
killers with guns

b
police officers

c
a shark

d
a plane

e
drugs

f
money

West Palm Beach marina

'We're free for five days. It's wonderful,' said Greg happily.

'Yes, but don't forget about the **exam** next week,' said Jessica. 'I *must* **study**. I don't know anything!'

All the friends looked at Jessica and then they looked down at their feet. It was true. Five days' **vacation** was wonderful but nobody wanted to study for all that time.

'Well, I'm not going to study. I'm going to do something different,' said Matt suddenly.

His friends looked at him. 'I'm not going to sit here at **college** for five days. What's wrong with everybody? Let's have a good time.'

'Matt's right,' said Amy. 'Let's do something different; something exciting!'

exam a student takes these to see how much he or she knows

study to learn about something

vacation days when you do not have to go to school

college a place where students go to study when they finish high school

'So what do you want to do, Amy – go **scuba diving** in the Bahamas or something?' asked Greg.

'Well, why not?' Amy answered quickly. 'It's more interesting than staying here.'

'OK,' laughed Jessica. 'You two can go off and do exciting things. I'm going to my room.'

One by one, the friends got up and left. The two friends sat and looked out of the window. They could see more college buildings and more students. Matt spoke first.

'Well Amy. What shall we do? Shall we drive down to West Palm Beach?'

'OK. Let's do that.'

Two hours later, the two friends walked slowly through the town and down to the **ocean**. It was late and there were not many people on the streets. They could hear the ocean and they could feel the warm **air** on their faces. They walked for a long time without speaking and then they arrived at the **marina**. There were a lot of big white **boats** there. They moved slowly up and down on the dark water. The two friends walked past the boats. Suddenly Matt stopped next to one of the biggest boats.

'Hey! Amy! This is my boat – let's get on it. We can go to any country we want!'

'Oh, Matt. Don't be **stupid**. You don't have a boat. I know that.'

'OK, but let's have a look at it. Perhaps we can take it to – oh, I don't know – South America or Europe or, or . . . Africa!

Matt **jumped** onto the **deck** of the big boat and, a minute later, Amy jumped after him. They laughed and

scuba diving swimming for a long time under the water

ocean sea

air we take this in through our mouth and nose

marina this is where small ships stay when they are not on the ocean

boat you go across water in this; a small ship

stupid not thinking well

jump to move fast on your legs from one thing to a different thing

deck where you walk on a boat

walked up and down the deck in the dark; they liked looking at all the things on that beautiful white boat.

'These people are rich,' said Amy. 'Perhaps they're famous too.'

'Sssh!' said Matt suddenly. 'Listen. I can hear something.'

The two friends said nothing. They could hear **voices** in the night air and they were very **close**. They got down on the deck behind some **oxygen tanks** at the front of the boat. The voices came closer and the friends felt afraid. Then some people got on the back of the boat. They could hear different men's voices and then the voice of a woman.

voice the noise that someone makes when they speak

close near

oxygen tank something with air in it that you wear on your back for scuba diving

'Let's get off, before they find us,' said Matt quietly into Amy's ear.

'But they're going to see us,' said Amy.

'It doesn't matter. Run fast and jump off. Quick!'

But before the two friends could move, something happened. Matt could see the people on the boat now and they were very close. There were three men and a woman and they were all angry. Amy and Matt watched. Then one of the men took out a **gun**. But before he could do anything, the woman took out her gun and **shot** him. With a cry, the man's body went down into the water.

'Why did you do that, Sharon?' cried one of the men angrily. 'We needed Luis for the **dive**!'

'Be quiet, Troy,' answered the woman. 'We couldn't **trust** him. You know that. We can think about the dive later.'

'Come on – let's go!' said Troy. 'We don't want the **police** to get here and begin running all over the boat.'

They began to move. The second man ran to the front of the boat but he did not see Matt and Amy behind the oxygen tanks. Troy and Sharon went into the **cabin** at the back of the boat.

'Matt,' said Amy, 'I'm **scared**. What's happening? Who are these people?'

'I don't know but they're **dangerous**. Let's get out of here.'

Just then, the boat began to move under their feet. Slowly it moved away from the boats next to it in the marina. Amy looked at Matt. His mouth was open and his eyes were scared and Amy felt scared too. They could not get off the boat. Nobody could help them now.

gun a person can fight with this

shoot (*past* **shot**) to use a gun

dive when you swim down under water; to swim under water

trust to think that someone is working with you

police they find people who do something bad

cabin a room on a boat

scared afraid

dangerous that can kill you

In her room at Florida Atlantic College, Jessica felt tired. It was late and she did not want to study. She made a cup of coffee and took it into a big room downstairs. The students usually met to talk there. A minute later Greg came into the room. He smiled at her.

'I can't study, Jess. Do you have that problem, too?'

'Yes. Matt and Amy were right. We can't study all the time! Did they go out?'

'Yes. I heard Matt's car at about ten o'clock.'

They looked at the clock and said nothing. It was after one o'clock in the morning. Suddenly Jessica spoke. 'Well, perhaps they found something exciting to do out there,' she said, and she laughed.

READING CHECK

What do they say?

1 'What do you want to do – go scuba diving in the Bahamas or something?'

2 'I must study. I don't know anything!'

3 'Listen. I can hear something.'

4 'Let's get out of here.'

5 'We needed Luis for the dive.'

6 'Perhaps they found something exciting to do out there.'

7 'We couldn't trust him.'

8 'Don't be stupid. You don't have a boat.'

a Jessica says to her friends: ☐ 2

b Greg says to Amy: ☐

c Amy says to Matt at the marina: ☐

d Matt says to Amy on the boat: ☐

e Troy says to Sharon after she shoots Luis: ☐

f Sharon says to Troy: ☐

g Matt says to Amy just before the boat begins to move: ☐

h Jessica says to Greg later that night at college: ☐

WORD WORK

1 Complete the sentences with the pairs of words.

| scared / dangerous | exam / vacation | trust / shoots | voice / close | deck / air |

a Suddenly Matt hears a man's .... voice ......, very ..... close ..... to him.

b Sharon doesn't .... Luis, so she .... him.

c Amy feels .... to be on the boat with three .... people.

d We sat on the .... of the boat, having a drink and feeling the warm .... on our faces.

e After I finish my .... I'm going to have a long .... in the Bahamas.

2 Match the words with the pictures.

a 4

b

c

d

e

f

1 college
2 ocean
3 cabin
4 jump
5 oxygen tank
6 gun

STINGRAY

GUESS WHAT

What happens in the next chapter? Tick three boxes.

a ☐ Amy and Matt jump off the boat.

b ☐ Troy hears Matt's phone.

c ☐ Sharon wants to shoot Matt and Amy.

d ☐ Sharon takes Amy and Matt back to the marina.

e ☐ Troy throws Matt off the boat.

f ☐ 'Perhaps these two can help us,' says the second man.

Deep trouble

The boat moved through the marina and out into the open ocean.

Amy spoke first. 'Oh, help! Where are we going? What are we going to do?'

'Let's speak to these people,' said Matt. 'We can say "sorry" and leave. They don't want us here. We're close to the marina. Perhaps they can go back and leave us there.'

'They aren't going to take us back, Matt. What happened to that man? They shot him. These people are bad. We don't want them to shoot us, too.'

'Well, what can we do, Amy? We can't stay here. They're going to find us soon.'

'I know! Let's jump off and **swim** back to the marina! It isn't far,' said Amy.

'In that dark water? The water's **deep** here, and it's dangerous. I'm going to call the police and get help.'

Matt took out his **cell phone**, but before he could call anybody the phone **rang**.

'Oh no, somebody's calling *me*!'

'Quickly, stop that noise—'

But before Matt could stop it, a man's voice came out of the night.

'Hey! What's that noise?'

They heard his feet on the deck. Quickly he came closer. Now he stood over them. It was Troy. He **shouted** to Sharon and the second man:

'Hey **guys**, I don't like to say this, but we have a **problem**. Look here!' His hand moved quickly. He took

swim (*past* **swam**) to move through the water

deep many metres down

cell phone a telephone that you can take with you

ring (*past* **rang**) to make a noise; a telephone makes this noise when somebody calls

shout to say noisily and angrily

guy person

problem something that is difficult

Matt's phone and **threw** it into the water.

In seconds Sharon arrived. She had her gun in her hand.

'What are you two doing here? Come on, talk!' she said angrily.

'N-nothing,' said Amy. 'We wanted to see the boat. That's all.'

'Oh yes? That's a good story! Let's go! Move!'

They **pushed** Amy and Matt into the cabin at the front of the boat. The second man was there. He was the driver of the boat.

'Look Brad,' said the woman. 'These two were on the boat all the time. They saw everything.'

'No!' said Matt quickly. 'No, we didn't see a thing. Look, please, can we go? We aren't going to talk. We want to go home – that's all.'

throw (*past* **threw**) to make something move quickly through the air with your hand

push to move someone quickly and strongly with your hands

in deep trouble
with big problems

kid a young
person

drugs something
that people take
to make them feel
happy or excited

'You're **in deep trouble**, **kids**,' the woman said, and she looked at the two men. 'They saw everything. I'm going to shoot them.'

'Sharon's right,' said Troy. 'We can't trust them.'

Brad looked at the scared kids.

'Wait a minute. Perhaps these two can help us.' He looked at Matt. 'Hey, you, kid. Can you swim?'

'Yes, yes, I can. And Amy too. We're good swimmers. We can swim back to the marina. No problem.'

'To the marina? You *are* good swimmers! Can you dive too?' Brad asked.

'Dive? Yes. But why . . . ?' Matt began to feel afraid. What did this man want from him?

Brad spoke to Sharon and Troy.

'Look, we don't have Luis with us now and he was our diver. This kid can help us to bring up the **drugs**. His

girlfriend isn't going to do anything stupid when he's under the water.'

Troy spoke; 'I don't like it. I can dive, and I don't need help from some kids.'

'Listen, you're not a good diver, Troy. Luis was the man for that and he's not here.'

'It's true, Troy,' said the woman. 'The kid can do it. You can go down with him to help him!' She laughed.

'OK then,' said Troy and he looked at Sharon angrily. 'Let's put them in the small cabin for now. When we get to the Bahamas they can come out again. Come on, you two – move.'

Sharon and Troy took Amy and Matt along the deck to the cabin at the back of the boat. They pushed them in and Sharon put the gun next to Matt's head.

'Be careful,' she said. 'Luis was stupid. He told the police about us and so he died. Do something stupid and that can happen to you, too.'

Sharon and Troy left the cabin and closed the door. Matt and Amy heard the **key** in the door, then the noise of feet on the deck, and then nothing.

Matt waited a minute before he spoke.

'What are we going to do, Amy? These people are **drug traffickers**!'

'Yes, and you're going to help them to find their drugs!'

'But why are the drugs under the ocean in the Bahamas?'

'Why is that important? These people want to kill us! We must get away from them!'

'No. Amy, let's sit here quietly for now. They need me for the dive. We have time to think of something before then.'

'OK,' said Amy, but she was very scared.

key you can close or open a door with this

drug trafficker a dangerous person who buys and sells drugs

11

READING CHECK

Are these sentences true or false? Tick the boxes.

		True	False
a	Amy wants to swim back to the marina.	☑	☐
b	Matt calls a friend on his cell phone.	☐	☐
c	Brad throws Matt's phone into the water.	☐	☐
d	At first Sharon wants to shoot Amy and Matt.	☐	☐
e	Matt is a good diver.	☐	☐
f	The boat is going to Cuba.	☐	☐
g	Sharon puts her gun next to Amy's head.	☐	☐
h	Matt wants time to think.	☐	☐

WORD WORK

1 These words don't match the pictures. Correct them.

a ~~throw~~
..swim..

b swim

. . . .

c push

. . . .

d ring

. . . .

e shout

. . . .

2 Find words from Chapter 2 in the ocean.

keykidguyproblemdeepdrugtraffickersdeeptrouble

3 Use the words from Activity 2 to complete the sentences.

a 'Who's the .... *guy* .... with the short hair and the black shirt?'

b 'Don't jump in the river here; it's very . . . .'

c 'The police at the marina are always looking for . . . .'

d 'We can't open the door – we don't have the right . . . .'

e 'Don't be angry with your little brother – he's just a . . . .'

f 'I broke my sister's computer. Oh no, I'm in . . . . !'

g 'So there are six people and only four chairs? Hmm – we have a . . . .'

GUESS WHAT

What happens in the next chapter? Tick the boxes.

a Matt and Amy's friends . . .
   1 ☐ look for Matt and Amy.
   2 ☐ phone the police.
   3 ☐ study for their exams.

b Matt . . .
   1 ☐ dives for the drugs.
   2 ☐ fights Troy.
   3 ☐ swims away when no one is looking.

c Troy . . .
   1 ☐ dives with Matt.
   2 ☐ stays on deck with Sharon.
   3 ☐ waits in the water for the drugs.

d Amy . . .
   1 ☐ cries because she is scared.
   2 ☐ goes diving with Matt.
   3 ☐ stays on the boat with Sharon and Brad.

Diving for their lives

The next day, Jessica got up late and went downstairs to have breakfast. She saw her friends Greg and Tom at one of the tables, and she sat down next to them.

'Hi. Where is everybody?'

'You're late, Jess,' said Greg. 'Everybody's in their rooms now, and they're all studying.'

'Well, not all of them. Some are playing tennis,' laughed Tom. 'See you later!'

'What about Amy and Matt?' asked Jessica.

'Perhaps they went to visit Matt's Dad in Jacksonville,' said Greg. 'Matt wanted to see him.'

'Or perhaps they're somewhere in the Bahamas, swimming and **sunbathing**,' said Jessica, and she smiled.

'Wonderful! I would like to be there now,' said Greg.

'Well, let's go – after the exams!' said Jessica.

Matt and Amy slept very badly in the little cabin. There was not much air and they were hungry and thirsty. In the morning Amy looked at her watch. It was nine o'clock.

'How far is it to the Bahamas, Matt? How many hours?' she asked.

'I don't know. Not far.'

Half an hour later, Troy came with some water but he did not bring any food. He didn't speak to them, and they were afraid to ask questions.

Some time later, the boat stopped. The cabin door opened for the second time and Sharon came in with some bread and some cold meat. Matt and Amy ate hungrily. Sharon

sunbathe to sit in the sun

said nothing but watched them carefully. Then she spoke to Matt.

'That's right, kid. Eat! You need to feel good for the dive.'

'Am I going to dive for drugs?'

'That's right. There are some **packages** down there – twenty of them. In these packages there are some very good drugs and they're going to make us very rich. Oh, yes! They're going to make me and my friends a lot of money.' Sharon thought of all the money and smiled.

'Why are they under the ocean?' asked Matt.

'They were on a boat from the south. The police came onto the boat so our friends threw the packages into the water. But we know where they are – and you're going to get them for us,' said Sharon.

package you put something in this to carry or send it easily

'What about me? What am I going to do?' asked Amy.

'You kids ask a lot of questions,' said Sharon angrily. 'You, girl, are going on deck with me and Brad. We're going to have a nice family day out on the boat – Mom, Dad, and daughter. You're going to do nice things: drink Coke, listen to music and sunbathe. Your boyfriend – no, your brother – is going to go scuba diving with his Uncle Troy. He doesn't like sunbathing. Do you understand?'

'Yes,' said Amy.

'Right – now get on deck. And remember, I'm watching you, do you hear?'

Sharon put her hand on the gun in her pocket, and pushed Amy and Matt out of the door.

On deck, the sun was high in the sky and it was hot. Far away they could see a white **beach** and some trees. The ocean was a beautiful blue colour.

Troy spoke to Matt.

'Right, kid. I'm going into the water with you, but you are going to dive. When you find something, bring it to me – understand?'

'Yes.'

Troy and Matt got ready for the dive. Matt put on a **wet suit**; the wet suit of the dead man, Luis. Matt felt **strange**. He put the oxygen tank on his back. It felt **heavy** out of the water. Soon Troy and Matt were ready. Sharon and Brad sat on the deck with Amy between them. Sharon wore dark **glasses** and had a camera in her hand.

'Amy is going to be right here with us all the time,' said Sharon. 'Remember that, Matt.'

Troy went into the water first. Then Matt went in. The water was not cold and for a minute Matt felt free and

beach near the ocean, where you sunbathe on vacation

wet suit you wear this for scuba diving

strange not usual

heavy difficult to carry

glasses you wear these in front of your eyes

happy. But Troy was next to him, and Sharon watched him from the boat. Matt thought about Amy and Sharon's gun. 'I'm diving for our lives,' he thought and went down to look for the packages.

From the deck, Amy thought about Matt. He was down for a long time and did not come up again. Was he OK?

'Smile, Amy,' said Sharon, and she took a photograph. 'You're on vacation!'

'Have a drink,' said Brad. He gave Amy a glass of Coke.

Amy could not take her eyes off the water. Where was Matt? Was there a problem? At that moment she saw his head but only for seconds. He gave something to Troy and then went down under the water again.

READING CHECK

1 Match the sentences with the people.

1 Matt

2 Sharon

3 Amy

4 Jessica

5 Troy

a ☐ 4 talks to Greg about Matt and Amy.

b ☐ brings the two friends some water.

c ☐ tells Matt to dive for the drugs.

d ☐ has to stay on deck with Sharon and Brad.

e ☐ stays in the water to help Matt.

f ☐ takes a photo of Amy.

g ☐ finds drugs under the water.

2 Correct the mistakes in these sentences.

a Matt and Amy sleep ~~well~~ *badly* in the little cabin.

b When the boat stops, Sharon brings them coffee and cold meat.

c There are twenty packages of money under the sea.

d The police threw the packages of drugs into the water.

e Amy is going to drink tea on the boat with Sharon and Brad.

f Sharon sits on the deck with a sun hat in her hand and a gun in her pocket.

g Amy sees Matt's back for a short time before he goes down again.

WORD WORK

1 Find six more words from Chapter 3 on the beach.

r	s	t	r	a	n	g	e	u	v
s	u	y	m	w	q	l	p	n	x
l	n	p	a	c	k	a	g	e	j
v	b	t	q	z	y	s	b	f	e
o	a	h	c	n	p	s	e	g	r
y	t	a	u	i	h	e	a	v	y
l	h	b	i	r	t	s	c	p	d
w	e	t	s	u	i	t	h	x	o

2 Use the words from Activity 1 to complete these sentences.

a When I go on vacation I like to swim and sit on the . . . *beach* . . .

b When you go scuba diving, you wear a . . . . on your body.

c On a sunny day, dark . . . . are good for your eyes.

d 'I can't pick up this box – it's very . . . . !'

e When you go to a different country, everything looks . . . . to you at first.

f When you . . . . , the sun feels hot on your body.

g 'What's in that . . . . ?' 'Some books, I think.'

GUESS WHAT

What happens in the next chapter? Tick the boxes.

a Who comes near the boat?
  1 ☐ Some divers.
  2 ☐ The police.
  3 ☐ The Coast Guard.

b Who stops Amy when she starts to talk?
  1 ☐ Brad.
  2 ☐ Sharon.
  3 ☐ Troy.

c What does Troy want to do?
  1 ☐ Kill Amy and Matt.
  2 ☐ Send Amy and Matt home.
  3 ☐ Throw Amy and Matt in the water.

d What does Brad want to do?
  1 ☐ Leave Amy and Matt on the boat.
  2 ☐ Put Amy and Matt on a plane.
  3 ☐ Throw Amy and Matt in the water.

'Smile! You're on vacation!'

Matt went down again. How many packages did Troy have now? Eight? Nine? Matt felt tired and scared. Some of the things under the ocean were beautiful. There were **fish** of many different colours. But he only wanted to find the packages. Most of them were between the **rocks** and they weren't easy to find. Again and again, he went down and took the packages up to Troy. Amy, Sharon, and Brad watched from the deck.

'How many are there?' Matt asked. 'Is that it?'

'Two more and that's it,' said Troy.

At that moment, the three people on deck heard a noise. They could see a boat very close to them. When it began to come closer, Sharon said quietly, 'It's the **Coast Guard**. We're on vacation, remember. Smile and look friendly.' When she spoke, Sharon put her hand on Amy's arm and pushed down. Amy wanted to cry out but she said nothing.

The Coast Guard boat came very close. One of the men on it shouted; 'Hi, good morning. Is everything OK?'

'Wonderful. Thanks,' shouted Sharon.

Amy sat up suddenly and began to **wave**.

'Help! We're—' she began, but Brad pushed her arm down. Smiling, he spoke to her angrily.

'Don't be stupid, Amy. You don't want something to happen to your boyfriend.'

Amy looked down at the ocean and said nothing. Matt was under the water and Troy swam up and down slowly looking at the beautiful fish. The Coast Guard boat began to move away.

fish an animal that lives in water

rock fish and other ocean animals live on and between these under the ocean

Coast Guard they look after the ocean close to the beaches

wave to move your hand in the air

'Bye. Have a nice day,' one of the officers shouted.

Sharon and Brad smiled and waved. Amy sat and watched the little boat. It moved far away.

The last two packages were difficult to find. Matt looked for them for a long time. Up on deck, Amy watched the water, looking for Matt's head and the yellow oxygen tank. Matt found the last packages and took them up. He was very tired.

On deck there were now twenty packages. Everybody stood and looked at them.

'Are they OK?' asked Troy. 'Do they have water in them?'

'They're OK,' said Sharon. 'And they're going to make us very rich. Thanks for your help, kid.'

Matt looked down at the drugs. 'Can we go now?' he asked.

Sharon laughed. 'Are you **kidding**?' she said. 'You want to go home to Florida? But then you can tell all your college friends about us, and we don't want that. No, my friend. You're going to die. And your girlfriend, too.' She looked at Amy.

'Wait a minute, Sharon,' said Brad. 'Let's think. How are we going to take the drugs into the States? *We* can't do it. **Maybe** the police have Luis's body. They're going to ask a lot of questions about his friends. So maybe the kids can help us with this, too.'

'Brad,' said Troy angrily. 'I don't understand you. Why are you always interested in these kids? It's very strange. We have the drugs. Let's shoot them and forget about them. We can't trust them. They're going to speak to the police.'

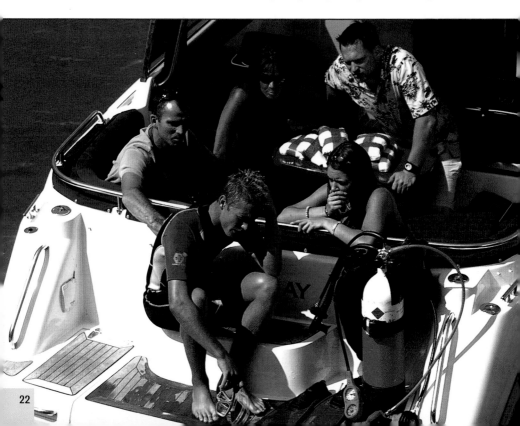

'Yes,' said Sharon. 'Why are Matt and Amy going to take the drugs into the States for us? They're going to give them to the police.'

'But we know all about their college friends,' said Brad. 'Amy told me all about Greg and Jessica. Oh, and you have a little sister; is that right, Matt? We know a lot about them. They don't want something bad to happen to their friends or their families.'

Amy began to cry. Matt was cold now after the dive and his face was white.

Sharon looked at them.

'OK. Maybe they can help us. Let's take them to Nassau. We can get **passports** for them there and put them on the plane. Then maybe we can stay on the boat and wait. When the drugs are in the States, we can kill the kids. Then they can't talk.'

'That's a stupid **idea**!' said Troy. 'Kill the kids now, and there's no problem!'

'No, Troy. *Think* for once. We need the drugs and the money. We can't go back to the States now because the police are looking for us. The kids are scared and they're going to do everything we tell them. Is that right?'

Sharon looked first at Matt and then at Amy. They did not answer. What could they say?

Brad took out his cell phone. 'It's time to phone J.T. in Nassau,' he said. 'He can bring a car to the boat and then take us to the hotel.'

'We're going to need a big car for all the drugs,' laughed Sharon.

'Yes, and for these two,' said Troy, and he looked at Matt and Amy darkly.

passport a book with your name and photograph; you take it with you when you visit different countries

idea a plan or a new thought

23

READING CHECK

Put these sentences in the correct order. Number them 1–8.

a ☐ Sharon says 'yes' to Brad's idea.

b ☐ Amy begins to talk to the Coast Guard.

c ☐ Sharon wants to kill Matt and Amy.

d ☐ The Coast Guard boat comes close.

e ☐ Brad tells J.T. to meet them in Nassau.

f ☐ Brad stops Amy from talking.

g ☐ Matt comes on deck with the last two packages.

h ☐ 'Perhaps Matt and Amy can take the drugs into the States,' says Brad.

WORD WORK

Use the words in the picture of the diver on page 24 to complete the sentences.

a When you are in trouble on a boat, you can call the . . Coast . . . .Guard. . .
for help.

b Matt does not have time to look at the beautiful . . . . in the water near him.

c Matt finds the last package of drugs under a . . . .

d There's somebody at the door; . . . . it's my brother.

e Your mother can't see us — . . . . your hand in the air!

f I'm not . . . ., I tell you – I can't find my money!

g At the airport somebody looks at your . . . . and your ticket.

h You want to go swimming? That's a good . . . .

GUESS WHAT

What happens in the next chapter? Tick the boxes.   **Yes**   **No**

a Matt and Amy jump out of J.T.'s car. ☐ ☐

b J.T. wants to kill Matt and Amy. ☐ ☐

c The police are looking for Luis's killers. ☐ ☐

d Troy wants to leave Nassau fast. ☐ ☐

e All the drugs are in Amy's bag. ☐ ☐

f Jessica and her friends see Amy and Matt on television. ☐ ☐

'Open your bag, please'

The marina at Nassau was hot and sunny. When they left the boat, Sharon walked behind Amy, and Troy walked next to Matt.

'There's J.T.' said Sharon.

A big black car waited not far from the boat. The driver wore a dark blue suit and dark glasses.

'Get in. Why are there five of you?' he asked.

'A good question,' said Troy angrily.

They got into the car. Brad sat in the front next to J.T. Sharon and Troy went in the back with Amy and Matt. Matt was between Amy and the window. He could see the streets and houses of Nassau on the road to the hotel. There was a **carnival** that day and the streets were full of people. The car stopped three or four times because there were people in front of them in the road. J.T. was angry.

'Move, you guys!' he shouted every time.

Once when they stopped, Matt spoke quietly to Amy.

'Next time we stop, let's open the door and jump out,' he said.

But Troy understood. 'Forget it, kid!' he said. 'You can't open the door. J.T. isn't stupid.'

Soon they arrived at the hotel. Sharon took Matt and Amy to their room.

'Sit down and don't open your mouths,' she said. She went to the television. 'Let's watch TV while we're waiting.'

Five minutes later, J.T., Brad and Troy came into the room. J.T. had a camera in his hand.

carnival a vacation for everybody when people wear wonderful things and move happily through the streets

'We need photos of these two for their passports,' he said. 'Smile!' He took some photographs, first of Amy and then of Matt. 'OK, I'm going now. Wait here and don't go out. You can ask for something to eat in the room.'

'When are you going to bring the passports?' asked Troy.

'Tonight. And the plane tickets too. The kids can go tomorrow.'

He left. For some time, the only noise in the room came from the television.

'. . . Police in West Palm Beach knew the man well. He was Luis Cortez, a drug trafficker. They are now looking for his killers. They were on a boat and they left the marina soon after . . .'

'They're talking about us! Let's get out of here!' shouted Troy.

'Take it easy,' said Brad. 'They didn't give any names.'

'Maybe they know our names but they're not saying,' said Sharon. 'Tomorrow when the kids are on the plane, let's go back to the boat and take it somewhere.'

'OK,' said Brad. 'But for now we wait here.'

The next morning, Amy and Matt stood in the hotel room ready to go to the airport. They had **false** passports and plane tickets to the United States. The packages of drugs were in two bags under some **clothes** and books. J.T. and Sharon drove them to the airport. Before they went over to the police with their passports, Sharon spoke to them for the last time: 'We have a man on the plane. Don't forget that. And someone is going to meet you when you arrive. Remember your friends and your families, and be careful. Goodbye. Have a nice day!'

Seventy minutes later, Amy and Matt were back in the United States. They showed their passports and walked through into **Customs**. It was then that everything began to go wrong.

'Open your bag please,' said the customs officer to Amy.

He looked in the bag under the clothes and books.

'Just a minute. What's this under here?' He opened one of the packages a little.

'Did you know about this?'

'Yes,' said Amy. 'But I can **explain**. They aren't our drugs. You see—'

'Open your bag too!' said the officer to Matt. 'Let me see . . . Hmm, you and your girlfriend have a problem here.'

'No, listen please. You see, we went to the marina at West

false not true

clothes people wear these

Customs when you go into a different country, officers look in your bags here

explain to tell the true story about something

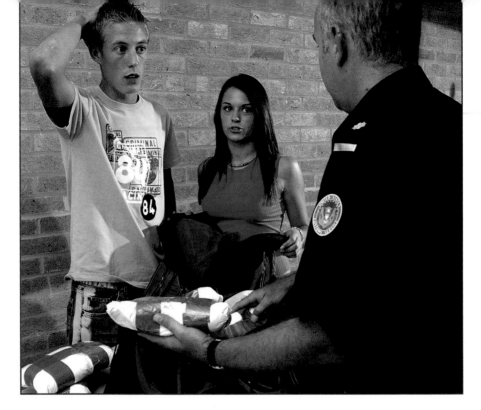

Palm Beach to see the boats and—'

'OK, OK. Forget the stories. Come with me. You can explain this to the airport police. You're in big trouble, kids.'

That night at Florida Atlantic College, Jessica, Greg, and their friends watched television with open mouths. They could not **believe** it – Amy and Matt were in **prison** for drug trafficking!

'It isn't true! Amy and Matt aren't drug traffickers. They need our help,' said Jessica.

'Yes, but what can we do?' said Greg.

'Hey, but look at all those drugs,' said Tom. 'How did they get into their bags?'

'I don't know,' said Jessica. 'But Amy and Matt didn't put them there. I know that.'

believe to think that something is true

prison a place where people stay when they do something wrong

READING CHECK

Match the first and second parts of these sentences.

a J.T. is waiting for them . . .

b Matt wants to jump . . .

c Sharon takes Matt and Amy . . .

d J.T. comes into the hotel room . . .

e The police are looking . . .

f The packages of drugs are . . .

g Back in the United States, Matt and Amy are . . .

h Jessica and Greg see Matt and Amy . . .

1 under some clothes and books.

2 on television.

3 with a camera in his hand.

4 in a big black car.

5 in big trouble.

6 for the killers of Luis Cortez.

7 to their room in the hotel.

8 out of the car.

WORD WORK

1 Complete the puzzle with words from Chapter 5.

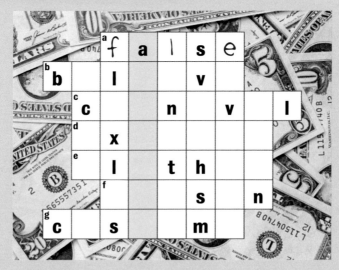

a f	a	l	s	e		
b b		l		v		
c c			n		v	l
d	x					
e	l		t	h		
f				s		n
g c		s		m		

2 Use the letters in the blue squares to make one more word. Amy and Matt go here with Sharon.

a _ _ _ _ _ _

3 Use the words from Activity 1 to complete these sentences.

a People are happy in Nassau because it is ⎯carnival⎯. time.

b J.T. gives Amy and Matt . . . . passports.

c The . . . . officer wants to look in Amy's bag.

d The drugs are under some . . . . and books.

e Amy wants to . . . . , but the officer starts to look in Matt's bag.

f The airport police take Matt and Amy to . . . .

g 'I don't . . . . it,' says Jessica. 'Matt and Amy aren't drug traffickers.'

GUESS WHAT

In the next chapter, someone helps Matt and Amy. Who is it?

Sharon ☐

Brad ☐

Troy ☐

J.T. ☐

the customs officer ☐

'Oh no! It's Brad!'

After their **arrest**, Amy and Matt explained everything to the police, but nobody believed their story. That night they were in different rooms of the prison. Amy was scared and she couldn't sleep. 'What's going to happen to us?' she thought. 'What's Sharon going to do when she finds out? What's going to happen to our friends? What are my mom and dad going to say?'

The next morning, a policeman took Amy to a sunny room with big windows. Matt was there. He was happy to see Amy, but he was **worried**.

'OK. Stay here,' said the policeman, and he left.

'I don't understand,' said Matt. 'Why are we here?'

'Yes, it's strange. Maybe our families are coming to visit us.'

'But Sharon and the others said—'

'Don't talk about it, Matt. I don't want to think about those people.'

'OK, Amy, but we did nothing wrong. The police don't believe that. So what can we say to them? We don't want to sleep here for a second night.'

'No! I want to sleep for a week – but not here!'

Just then, they heard a noise. The door opened and a man came into the room. He came closer and he smiled.

'Oh no,' said Amy. 'It's Brad!'

In her room at college, Jessica wanted to study but it was not easy. Again and again she thought of Matt and Amy and their problems. Her cell phone rang.

arrest the time when the police take someone to prison; to take someone to prison

worried not happy about something and thinking a lot about it

'Hello?' Jessica answered.

'Hello. Is this Jessica Lawson?'

'Yes?'

'Hi, Jessica. I write for the *Daily* **News**. How do you feel about the arrest of your two friends?'

'What? How did you get my number?'

'Tell me Jessica, were Matt and Amy drug traffickers or did someone put the drugs in their bags?'

'Look, I don't want to talk to you. Goodbye!' Angrily, Jessica threw the phone down.

A minute later, it rang again.

'Hello?'

'Good morning. Jessica? This is Chuck White of *Talk* **magazine**. What can you tell me about Matt and Amy? Are they very good friends or . . . ?'

Jessica threw the phone down again and sat down on her bed. When the phone rang for the third time, she did not answer it.

news stories about things that are happening now

magazine a thin book with news and lots of photos; you can buy it every week or every month

Back in the sunny room, Matt and Amy looked at Brad.

'W-What are you doing here?' asked Matt.

'It's OK, Matt. Hi, Amy.' Brad sat down and looked at the two scared friends. 'I'm an **undercover agent**,' he said.

'I don't believe you. You're a drug trafficker!' said Amy.

'No, I'm not. I work for the police.'

'I don't understand,' said Matt. 'Why didn't you help us? Why did you do all those things?'

'Yes, I'm sorry about all that. But I worked for months with the drug traffickers in different countries. There were more people than Sharon and Troy, and they did some very bad things. They trusted me. I wanted to wait and arrest them all with the drugs. But then you came and . . . things changed. I'm sorry about the dive Matt, but they wanted to kill you and it was the only thing to do.'

'But we took all those drugs on the plane,' cried Amy. 'That was your idea, too.'

'Yes, Amy, it was dangerous and I'm sorry, but it was the only answer. I couldn't do anything to help you then. I went back to the boat and waited. After your arrest I talked to the police. Before you could be free again, there were a number of arrests of important people in the Bahamas and here in the States. There were arrests in other countries, too. The police are very happy. A lot of very dangerous people are in prison now.'

'Yes, and we're in prison too,' said Matt. 'What about our families and our friends? What do they think of us now?'

'Take it easy,' smiled Brad. 'You and Amy are free to go now. And soon everybody is going to know the true story about your little vacation.'

The next day, Amy and Matt's story was in the **newspaper**.

undercover agent a policeman who does not wear policeman's clothes, so people do not know that he's working for the police

newspaper people read about things that happen every day in this

34

Students Free After Drug Arrest

STUDENTS OF **F**LORIDA Atlantic College, Matt Kreski and Amy Collins, 18, had an exciting vacation this week. They got on a boat at West Palm Beach and minutes later they were in deep trouble. It was a drug traffickers' boat and soon after Matt and Amy arrived, the traffickers got on the boat, shot a man, and left for the Bahamas. When they found Matt and Amy on their boat, they wanted to shoot them. But Matt is a good swimmer and diver, and the drug traffickers needed him. The young man dived and brought up twenty packages of drugs from the ocean. Amy watched Matt from on deck. When the Coast Guard came close to the boat Amy shouted for help, but the traffickers stopped her. Later, the traffickers took Amy and Matt to a hotel in Nassau and the next day the two young friends were on a plane back to the States. In their bags, they had the twenty packages of dangerous drugs. Customs found the packages and made an arrest at once. The young people were in prison when an undercover agent from the boat called the police, and explained the true story. Matt and Amy are now free to go back to their studies at college.

'I knew it! They didn't do it!' Jessica waved the newspaper in the air. 'Look everybody. They're free!'

The students ran up to Jessica. Everybody wanted to see the newspaper. Jessica and her friends were excited and happy.

'The newspaper doesn't tell us much,' said Greg. 'Why were they on the boat at West Palm Beach? Why did Matt help get the drugs from the ocean?'

'You can ask them now,' said Tom. 'They're coming through the door.'

Matt and Amy walked slowly into the room.

'Well, hello! Are you guys OK?' asked Jessica.

'Yes,' said Amy. 'We're OK. It's good to be back here!'

'Sit down and tell us all about it,' said Tom. 'Were you scared?'

'Why did you get on the boat?'

'Tell us about the dive, Matt.'

The students began to ask more and more questions. Matt put his hands in the air.

'Hey, guys, stop a minute, OK? We need to call our families and then get some sleep. We can tell you all about it later.'

'Yes,' said Amy. 'I don't want to think about it now.'

'Well, you had an exciting time, Amy,' said Jessica.

'Exciting?' answered Amy. 'I like things here better. **Boring** is good. Hey, Matt where are you going?'

'I'm going to my room,' said Matt smiling. 'I'm going to study. We have an exam tomorrow, remember?'

boring not interesting

ACTIVITIES

READING CHECK

Correct nine more mistakes in the summary of this chapter.

airport

Amy and Matt tell their story to the police at the ~~marina~~, but nobody believes it. They go

to different rooms in the prison. The next evening a policeman takes Amy to a dark room.

Matt is there, and he is worried to see her. Soon, somebody comes into the room — it's

Troy! He tells the two brothers, 'I'm an undercover agent. After your arrest, I talked to the

college, and there were a number of accidents in the Bahamas and the United States.'

In the end Amy and Matt go back to the college and see their teachers. They have lots of

questions to ask Amy and Matt, but Matt wants to swim before his exam the next day.

WORD WORK

Use the letters to make words and write the sentences.

a Did you hear the **eswn** ? Matt and Amy are in prison!

Did you hear the news? Matt and Amy are in prison!

b After their **srtare** Matt and Amy go to prison for the night.

....

c Amy and Matt's friends are **rdowrei** when they see them on TV.

....

d Our friends are free! Look — here's their picture in the **ppewseran** .

....

e Brad is not a drug trafficker – he is an **vcrednreuo tngae** and he works for the police.

. . . .

f Every month I get a football **zmgaanei** with photos and stories in it.

. . . .

g It's **gnibro** here – let's find a more exciting place.

. . . .

GUESS WHAT

What happens after the story ends? Choose from these ideas, or add your own.

a ☐ Sharon and Troy go to prison.

b ☐ Nobody sees J.T. again.

c ☐ The friends go to the Bahamas – for a vacation this time.

d ☐ Matt is going to be an undercover agent after college.

e ☐ You can see Matt and Amy's story at the cinema.

f ☐ A newspaper gives Matt and Amy a lot of money for their story.

g ☐ . . . .

h ☐ . . . .

Project A   *Brad's Diary*

1 Read this page from Brad's diary. Answer the questions below.

Thursday

27th
M A Y

Tonight we came on the boat at 10 p.m.
Everything was OK - but then Sharon was
angry with Luis. She shot him, and his body fell
in the water. We left West Palm Beach quickly,
because we didn't want the police to come.
Then we had more trouble. Troy found two kids
on the boat. Sharon wanted to kill them. But
the boy, Matt, can dive, so he's going to help us
in the Bahamas. The kids were scared, and I
was worried, but for now it's OK! What's going
to happen tomorrow? I must be very careful.

a When did Brad go on the boat?
b What did Sharon do and why?
c Why did they leave West Palm Beach quickly?
d What happened next?
e What is Matt going to do?
f How did the kids feel?
g How did Brad feel?
h What must Brad do now?

2 The next day Brad writes in his diary again. Use the words below to complete his sentences.

Friday

28th

M A Y

We arrived in the Bahamas. . . . .

We stopped near. . . . .

and the sun was . . . .

Matt and Troy went . . . .

and Matt went down . . . .

Sharon, Amy and I . . . .

Suddenly the Coast Guard . . . .

Amy wanted . . . .

but I . . . .

Now we are in a hotel . . . .

Tomorrow Matt and Amy are . . . .

so everything is OK – for now!

very hot.	for the packages.	came near our boat.
flying to the States	to talk to them	in Nassau.
		this morning.
a white beach	stopped her.	sat on deck.	into the water

3 Now write a page from Brad's diary about his visit to Matt and Amy in prison.

Project B   *On Vacation*

1 In the Bahamas people on vacation can do these things. Match the words with the
pictures. Use a dictionary to help you.

a ☐ windsurfing   c ☐ sailing   e ☐ birdwatching
b ☐ fishing   d ☐ surfing   f ☐ golf

2 Read about the Bahamas on page 43 and complete the table below.

Where are the islands?	
How many islands are there?	
What's the capital city?	
How warm is it?	
How many people live there?	
What language do they speak?	
What things can you do?	
How can you travel?	
What place can you visit?	
What can you see there?	
What happens in the streets and when?	

Come to The Bahamas

Visit the Bahamas in the Atlantic Ocean near Florida. There are 700 beautiful islands and only 304,000 people.

People in the Bahamas speak English. You can travel around the islands by car, bicycle and water taxi! It's always warm here – between 15 and 23 °C.

There are lots of things to do in the Bahamas. You can go sailing, swimming, fishing, diving and birdwatching, and you can play golf. In the capital city, Nassau, you can visit the old Nassau Prison and see the old prisoners' rooms there. But it isn't a prison today – it's a museum!

On 26 December and 1 January you can see the Junkanoo – a big carnival in the streets of Nassau.

The Bahamas –
for a wonderful vacation!

3 Now use the notes from this table to complete the sentences about the Seychelles on page 44.

Where are the islands?	in the Pacific Ocean, near Madagascar
How many islands are there?	115
What's the capital city?	Mahé
How warm is it?	between 24 and 32 °C
How many people live there?	81,000
What languages do they speak?	Creole, English and French
What things can you do?	surfing, sailing, fishing, diving, tennis
How can you travel?	by car and bicycle
What place can you visit?	the National Museum of History in Mahé
What can you see there?	an old map of the Seychelles from 1517
What happens in the streets and when?	the FetAfrika, a carnival on 25 May

The Seychelles

The **Number 1** islands for vacations

Take your next vacation in the Seychelles.

The Seychelles are in the . . . . ,
near . . . .

. . . . people live on the
. . . . islands of the Seychelles.

People in the Seychelles speak . . . . You can travel by
. . . . and . . . . when you're there.
It's always warm in the Seychelles – between . . . .

There are lots of things to do in the Seychelles. Do you like the water? You can go
. . . . You can play . . . . too. In the capital
city, ... , you can go to the . . . .
There you can see . . . . from 1517.

On . . . . you can see the . . . . – a big
carnival on the streets of Mahé.

See you soon, in the Seychelles!

4 **Which islands (or island) you would like to visit on vacation? Write about them.**

Modal auxiliary verbs: must

We use must + infinitive without *to* when we think it is necessary or very important to do something, or when it is an obligation.

I must study. I don't know anything!   *'You must be quiet!' said Sharon.*

1 Complete the sentences with *must* and one of the verbs from the box.

bring	get off	go	kill	listen	look	take	wait

a We _must get off_ the boat before those people find us!

b Come on! We .... before the police get here.

c Dive down and when you find something, you
.... it to me.

d You .... happy, Amy. You're on holiday!

e We .... the kids now, then they can't speak to the police.

f I .... some photos of the kids for their passports.

g J.T., you .... for us at the marina in Nassau.

h 'Please, Officer, you .... ,' said Amy. 'These aren't our drugs.'

2 Imagine you are Amy or Matt. Write a sentence using *must* for each situation.

a You have an exam next week.
(study)   _I must study a lot this weekend._

b You see Sharon kill Luis with a gun.
(tell / police)   ....

c The boat starts moving out of the marina.
(jump / water)   ....

d A man is looking for you on the boat.
(be / quiet)   ....

e There is a Coast Guard boat near you.
(shout / for help)   ....

f You are in the car driving through Nassau.
(jump out)   ....

GRAMMAR CHECK

Going to Future: affirmative and negative

We make the *going to* future with the verb be + going to + infinitive.

We can use the *going to* future for intentions and plans.

I'm not going to sit here at college for five days.

We can also use the *going to* future for predictions.

They aren't going to take us back to the marina, Matt.

not answer / the phone	not go on a boat / again	arrest / drug traffickers	be / in prison / for years	not / have / a lot of money

a Jessica

b Amy

c Brad

d Sharon

e Troy

3 What are these people from the story going to do? Write sentences.

a <u>She isn't going to answer the phone.</u>

b ....

c ....

d ....

e ....

4 Write Matt's and Amy's questions using *going to*.

a When / we / arrive in / the Bahamas?

<u>When are we going to arrive in the Bahamas?</u>

b Why / I / dive / in the ocean? .... ?

c What / I / do? .... ?

d How long / we / stay in this hotel? .... ?

e Who / help / us? .... ?

f What / our parents / say? .... ?

g How / we / get out of / prison? .... ?

GRAMMAR CHECK

Present Simple and Present Continuous

We use the Present Simple to talk about facts that are always true, habits, and routines.

Where do they study?   *Amy and Matt study at Atlantic College, Florida.*

We use the Present Continuous to talk about actions happening at the time of speaking.

What are our friends doing?   *They're studying.*

5 Complete the gaps with the words in the box.

are	is	am	does	doesn't	do	~~don't~~

a Oh, Matt. Don't be stupid. You ..don't.. have a boat!

b I'm scared! Why .... he looking at us?

c What .... Sharon do? She's a drug trafficker.

d Sorry, but I can't talk now. I............ studying.

e Where .... Matt's parents live?

f Matt is a good diver, but he .... go diving very often.

g Maybe Matt and Amy .... swimming in the Bahamas right now.

6 Put the verbs in Brad's report into the Present Simple or the Present Continuous.

I a) ..'m working. (work) as an undercover agent with some drug traffickers. At the moment I b) .... (go) to the Bahamas on a boat with Sharon and Troy. Sharon c) .... (come) from New York. She's a very dangerous woman. She d) .... (work) with drug traffickers all over the world. Right now she e) .... (talk) to someone in the Bahamas on her cell phone. Troy sometimes f) .... (work) with Sharon as a diver. He g) .... (swim) every day but he h) .... (not / dive) very well. At the moment he i) .... (sit) on the deck with the two kids. They j) .... (not / talk). I k) .... (wait) to arrest Sharon and Troy, and I l) .... (want) to help the kids.

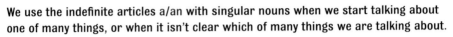

Articles: a/an, the

We use the indefinite articles **a/an** with singular nouns when we start talking about one of many things, or when it isn't clear which of many things we are talking about.

Matt stopped next to a boat. (There are lots of boats and he stopped next to one.)

We use **an** with singular nouns that start with a vowel sound.

They had an exam the next day. (One of many exams.)

We use the definite article **the** with singular and plural nouns when it is clear which thing we mean, or because the thing was already talked about.

Matt jumped onto the boat. (We already talked about it.)

We stood on the deck. (A boat only has one deck, so it is clear which we mean.)

7 Complete Amy's email to her parents with *a* or *the*.

We went for a) ..ᵃ.. walk near West Palm Beach marina. Matt saw b) ...... big boat and we jumped onto c) ...... deck to look at it. Then we heard d) ...... woman's voice. This woman took out e) ...... gun and shot f) ...... man. We wanted to jump off g) ...... boat, but it started to move. Matt wanted to call for help but h) ...... man came and threw Matt's cell phone into i) ...... water. He took us to j) ...... cabin at k) ...... front of the boat. l) ...... woman and m) ...... tall man were there. They took us to n) ...... smaller cabin and went out and closed o) ...... door.

8 Read the sentences and add *a* or *the* where necessary.

a Sharon opened <u>the</u> door, turned on <u>the</u> light, and walked in.

b 'Can I ask question, please?' said Matt.

c The police came onto boat and so friends threw packages into water.

d We're going to have nice family day on boat.

e At that moment people on deck heard noise.

f J.T. can bring car to boat and then take us to hotel.

GRAMMAR

GRAMMAR CHECK

Comparative and superlative adjectives

	Comparative	Superlative
Short adjectives, such as *deep*	add –er *deeper*	add the + –est *the deepest*
Adjectives finishing in –e, such as *close*	add –r *closer*	add the + –st *the closest*
Adjectives finishing in a short vowel + consonant, such as *big*	double the last consonant add –er *bigger*	double the last consonant add the + –est *the biggest*
Adjectives finishing in consonant + –y, such as *dirty*	change y to i and add –er *dirtier*	change y to i and add the + –est *the dirtiest*
Longer adjectives, such as *worried*	add more *more worried*	add the most *the most worried*

9 Complete the sentences using a comparative adjective.

a Troy is a good diver but Matt is ..better.. .

b Sharon is rich, but she wants to be ....

c Brad's idea is interesting, but mine is ....

d It was hot in West Palm Beach, but in Nassau it's ....

e Brad is quite tall, but Troy is ....

f The oxygen tank was heavy, but the packages were ....

g Amy was worried when Matt was on the boat, but she was ....
when he was in the water.

10 Complete the sentences using a superlative adjective.

a They are very bad people. They are the worst people I know.

b The white boat is big. It's .... in the marina.

c All the drug traffickers are dangerous, but Sharon is ....

d The four friends at the college are all young, but Amy is ....

e The exam was very easy, it was .... this year.

f The night in prison was boring, it was .... of my life.

g The packages were all heavy, but the last package was ....

GRAMMAR

GRAMMAR CHECK

Linkers: so and because

We use **so** to link two sentences when the second sentence explains a result.

Matt and I wanted to do something different <u>so we drove to Palm Beach</u>.

(result of first part of sentence)

We use **because** to link two sentences when the second sentence explains a reason.

The friends were happy <u>because they had five days' vacation</u>.

(reason for first part of sentence)

11 **Match the sentence halves, then write full sentences using *so* or *because*.**

a Matt and Amy got down behind some oxygen tanks
......*because they heard voices near the boat.*......

b Troy found Matt and Amy on the boat ....
....

c Luis told the police about the traffickers ....
....

d Amy didn't say anything to the Coast Guard ....
....

e The packages of drugs are under the ocean ....
....

f Sharon and Troy want to kill Matt and Amy ....
....

g The customs officer finds the drugs in Matt's and Amy's bags ....
....

h The police don't believe Matt's and Amy's story ....
....

☐ Matt's cell phone rang.
☑ they heard voices near the boat.
☐ Sharon shot him.
☐ they put them in prison.

☐ she was afraid for Matt.
☐ he takes them to the airport police.
☐ drug traffickers threw them into the water.
☐ they know about the drugs and the dead man.

GRAMMAR CHECK

Past Simple: information questions

We use question words – *What, When, Where, Which, Who, Why, How, How much,*
How many, and *How long* – in information questions. We answer these questions by
giving information.

In these Past Simple questions most verbs take did + subject + infinitive without *to*.

Where did you get the drugs?

With the verb be, we make questions in the Past Simple with was/were + subject.

Why were you scared?   *Where was her gun?*

12 Write questions for Matt's answers using the question words in the box.

How many	What	When	How long
Where	Which	Who	~~Why~~

a (get on / boat)   *Why did you get on the boat?*
Because I wanted to look at it.

b (the woman / shoot)   ....
A man called Luis Cortez.

c (the drug traffickers / find you)   ....
When my cell phone rang.

d (wear / go diving)   ....
A wet suit and an oxygen tank.

e (packages of drugs)   ....
There were twenty.

f (stay / in Nassau)   ....
In a hotel.

g (stay / in prison)   ....
For one night.

h (the worst moment)   ....
After my dive when they wanted to kill us.

⫻DOMINOES THE STRUCTURED APPROACH TO READING IN ENGLISH⫻

Dominoes is an enjoyable series of illustrated classic and modern stories in four carefully graded language stages – from Starter to Three – which take learners from beginner to intermediate level.

Each *Domino* reader includes:

- a **good story** to read and enjoy
- **integrated activities** to develop reading skills and increase active vocabulary
- **personalized projects** to make the language and story themes more meaningful
- **seven pages of grammar activities** for consolidation.

Each *Domino* pack contains a reader, plus a MultiROM with:

- a **complete audio recording of the story**, fully dramatized to bring it to life
- **interactive activities** to offer further practice in reading and language skills and to consolidate learning.

If you liked this Level One *Domino*, why not read these?

From the Heart
Alan C. McLean

Anna is a new student at Oxford University. When she arrives in Oxford, she meets Selim, and they become good friends. But Selim is not English, and living in a different country is not easy for him. Anna tries to help – but she knows that her father isn't going to like it.

Selim and Anna have each other. But is that enough? And can they find true happiness together?

Book ISBN: 978 0 19 424763 4
MultiROM Pack ISBN: 978 0 19 424727 6

The Wild West
John Escott

How much do you know about the Wild West? What do you know about cowboys and Indians, about wagon trails and gunfights?

Inside this book you will find the true story of the Wild West, and of some of the famous people who lived and worked there. People like Wyatt Earp, Jesse James, Billy the Kid – and Annie Oakley, the best shot in the West.

Book ISBN: 978 0 19 424769 6
MultiROM Pack ISBN: 978 0 19 424733 7

You can find details and a full list of books in the *Dominoes* catalogue and Oxford English Language Teaching Catalogue, and on the website: www.oup.com/elt

Teachers: see www.oup.com/elt for a full range of online support, or consult your local office.

	CEFR	Cambridge Exams	IELTS	TOEFL iBT	TOEIC
Level 3	B1	PET	4.0	57-86	550
Level 2	A2–B1	KET-PET	3.0-4.0	–	–
Level 1	A1–A2	YLE Flyers/KET	3.0	–	–
Starter & Quick Starter	A1	YLE Movers	–	–	–